on the farm

A FIRST PICTURE DICTIONARY

Words by Alison Wright

Pictures by Gerald Hawksley

On the farm

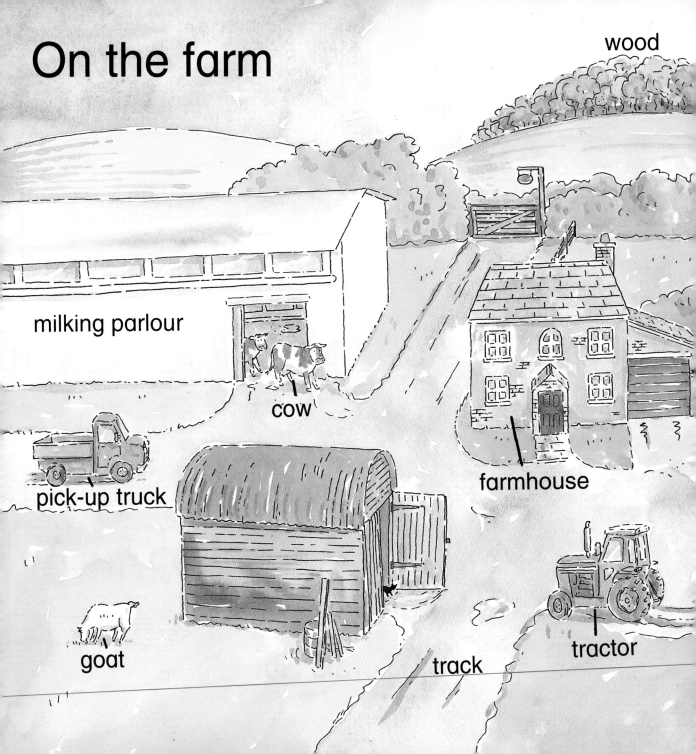

wood

milking parlour

cow

pick-up truck

farmhouse

goat

tractor

track

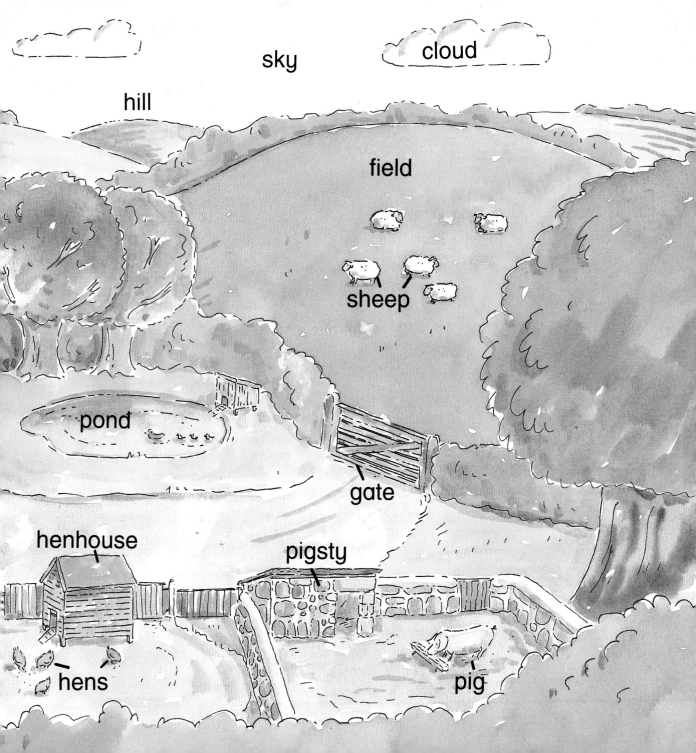

Sheep

baa!

woolly coat

hooves

Baby sheep are called lambs.

Sheep give us wool.

Sheep live in fields.

They eat grass.

Pig

curly tail

snout

oink!

trotters

Baby pigs are called piglets.

trough

Pigs eat a lot!

They live in pigsties.

Cow

horns

moo!

udder

Cows live in fields
and eat grass.
A group of cows is
called a herd.

Cows give us
milk, cheese
and yoghurt.

A baby cow
is called
a calf.

Horse

mane

neigh!

Horses can be ridden, and taught to jump. Some people jump horses in shows.

riding hat

jodhpurs

saddle

reins

riding boot

stirrup

horse shoe

Goat

bleat!

horns

beard

billy goat

Cheese and yoghurt can be made from goat's milk.

Goats will try to eat anything!

nanny goat

A baby goat is called a kid.

Hen

Duck

cluck!

quack!

comb

beak

wattle

bill

webbed feet

Baby hens are called chicks.

Hens and chicks eat worms and grain.

Hens give us eggs.

Ducks use their webbed feet to swim.

Baby ducks are called ducklings.

Sheepdog

woof!

Sheepdogs are trained to round up sheep.
They have to be very clever and obedient.

shepherd

pen

crook

Cat

Baby cats are called kittens. They love to play.

Farm cats are useful for catching rats and other vermin.

Cats like to sleep in the sun.

Tractor

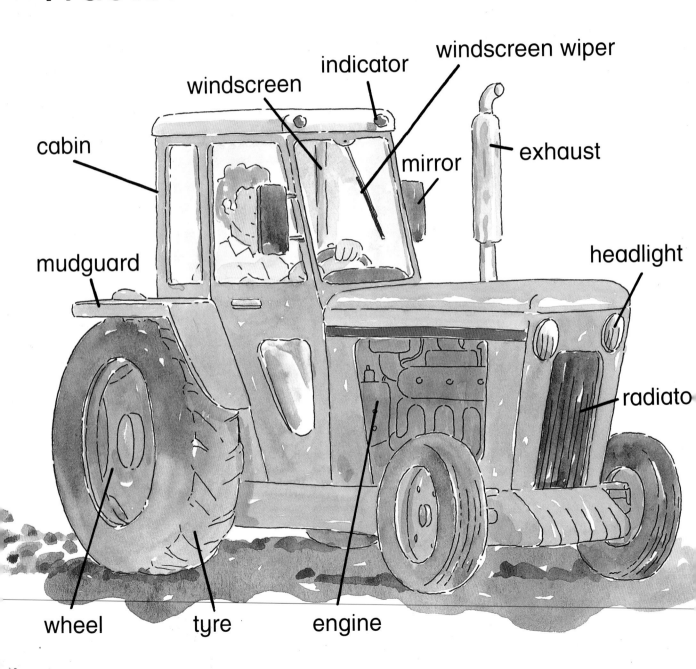

windscreen wiper

indicator

windscreen

exhaust

cabin

mirror

headlight

mudguard

radiato

wheel   tyre   engine

Tractors do most of the heavy work on the farm.

They pull trailers...

...and ploughs.

They help sow seed...

...and cut grass.

Their powerful engines and big wheels mean they can work in all types of weather.

Harvest time

combine
harvester

corn

poppy

straw

Pick-up truck

spare wheel

fog light

sack

tailgate

Four-wheel drive means they can climb steep hills and drive across muddy fields.

The pick-up truck does a lot of the fetching and carrying work on the farm.

All four wheels are driven by the engine giving better grip.

Milk tanker

How milk gets from the
the cow to you...

cow

The cow is milked
in the milking parlour.

The milk tanker collects
the milk and takes it to...

where milk is
bought, to be
drunk by...

...You!

the factory, where it is
put into cartons...

which are put
into trucks...

and taken
to shops...

Farm jobs

Here are some of the jobs a farmer might do.
Can you think of any others?

mending fences

feeding the pigs

mucking out stables

milking the cows

stacking bales

shearing sheep

collecting eggs

fixing the tractor

Wildlife

All these animals live
on, or near, a farm.
Some can be a nuisance
to the farmer.

owl

squirrel

fox

mouse

rat

rabbit